THE MOST AMAZING SOCCER STORIES OF ALL TIME

FOR KIDS!

MICHAEL LANGDON

itsmikelangdon

Dedication

To Tills, Charlie, Lily & Poppy with love.
Thank you for the inspiration.

A Free Gift For You

Thanks for buying this book!
As a special gift, you can also get the audiobook for free.
It's really fun to listen to the stories while you read along!

Just ask a grown-up to help you scan the QR code below
and enjoy the adventure!

FREE AUDIOBOOK

Before You Start

This book is produced with 🧡 for children everywhere in the USA.

As it was originally written for a global audience, you will find that we call soccer "football" throughout the book.

Please know that we mean soccer in those instances - the same beautiful game that unites us all.

Table of Contents

The Tiny Bird With Bent Legs

Once upon a time, in the land of magical footballers (Brazil), a small boy was born. The boy was so small that he looked like a wren.

A wren is one of the smallest birds to live on planet Earth. And this boy was so incredibly tiny, that his parents called him "Tiny Little Wren," Or "Garrincha," in his native Portuguese.

Garrincha wasn't like the other boys. Not only was he tiny, but he also had one leg that was bent, and it was much shorter than his other leg.

It seemed as if his small stature and bent legs would stop him from achieving his dream of playing football. However, his passion for football was so strong that he achieved some of the most incredible feats ever seen in the sport!

"Garrincha could do things with the ball that no other player could," said Pele, the best player of all time.

Garrincha went on to become one of the most feared footballing players of his time, leading Brazil to the 1958 and 1962 World Cup titles and being named player of the tournament AND top scorer in the 1962 World Cup.

Garrincha had it all. The Chilean journalists at the 1962 world cup were so impressed by his football ability, that they thought he actually came from another planet!

Off the football pitch he also did extraordinary things. One of the things he is famous for is having 22 children!

CBD

That's Just Scilly! The World's Smallest Football League

There is a tiny group of islands in the southwest of England called the Scilly Isles - it is home to only 2000 people.

Their love for football on the island is so strong that they started a football league - with only two teams in it!

And while the football might not be of the same standard as the Premier League, the Scilly Isles football league offers its own brand of charm.

The league competition involves the Woolpack Wanderers and the Garrison Gunners playing each other 18 times throughout the season.

It may not be the most exciting league in the world, but the beauty of this competition is that if you play for one of the teams, there is always a 50/50 chance of becoming champions of Scilly!

Games are often on a Sunday, and luckily for the players who don't like travelling, the games are always on the same pitch.

Another perk of playing football in the Scilly Isles, is that if at any time one of the teams is running away with the league, then there are always cup competitions to look forward to.

Two domestic cup competitions (The Wholesalers Cup and the Foredeck Cup) also take place in Scilly, and the long and arduous route to the final is always contested by the same two teams.

As if that wasn't enough, the football association of Scilly also puts on a Charity Shield competition as the season's first game.

And the two teams to compete in the Charity Shield? You guessed it. Woolpack Wanderers and the Garrison Gunners.

A Rush of Blood to The Head

This is the story of Zinedine Zidane's last ever game of football.

Zizou, as he was affectionately called, had the craziest final game of any football player in the world.

The biggest game in world football comes round once every four years. It is the World Cup final, and one BILLION people watch the game live.

In the final of Germany 2006, Zizou scored a 'Panenka' penalty kick.
A Panenka is a cheeky and unexpected dink of the ball that only the bravest of footballers ever dare to think about, let alone execute.

That alone would be reason to celebrate the day. But it is what happened a few minutes later that will forever be remembered.

With Italy and France tied at 1-1, and the game just about to go to penalties, Italian defender Marco Materazzi and Zinedine Zidane had a coming together on the pitch. Nothing unusual - just part of the game.

A few words were spoken, and BANG! Zizou exploded in a fit of anger.

In what can only be described as the biggest "red-rag-to-a-bull" moment in football history, Zizou threw himself, head-first, into the chest of Materazzi.

The referee missed the incident but his assistant didn't. After a private chat between the two, the referee had no option but to send him off minutes before the penalty shootout.

10
23

Paul The Psychic Octopus

During the World Cup in South Africa in 2010, it wasn't a footballer who was the star of the show, it was a psychic octopus!

When it comes to guessing the future, there are many different methods that people use to try and predict the future. Some use tarot cards, others palm read, some even use tea leaves to guess what's ahead.

One of the most unusual methods is using an octopus.

Paul the psychic octopus became famous for his ability to correctly predict the outcomes of football matches, including the 2010 World Cup final in which Spain became champions.

So how did he do it? Paul, who lived in a tank in Germany, would be fed from two boxes that were draped in the flags of the countries that were playing a match that day.

Whichever box he opened first would be deemed as his prediction as to which country would win the game.

In July 2010, Germany were playing Spain in the semi-final of the World Cup. That morning, Paul chose to have his breakfast from a box draped in a Spanish flag instead of the one draped in the German flag - he broke millions of German hearts that morning.

Later on that day, and as foretold by one of the greatest psychics the world has ever seen, Germany went on to lose the semifinal 1-0.

Paul always guessed correctly during that World Cup. He had the finest performance of 2010, and won the hearts of millions of football fans on every continent on earth.

Deutschland
España

Absolutely M/Dental!

A referee in Denmark couldn't blow his whistle for full time after he misplaced something very important.

You would be forgiven for thinking that the referee lost his whistle, but no, it was actually his teeth that he lost!

As is often the case with older people, they need fake teeth to replace their real teeth. This happens when they haven't taken care of their teeth growing up.

These fake teeth are called dentures, and Danish referee Henning Erikstrup had a lovely pair of dentures.

One day, he was refereeing a game between Ebeltoft and Norager. As he was running to keep up with the players, his teeth flew out of his mouth!

In the time it took him to find his teeth and put them back in his mouth, Ebeltoft scored a last minute equaliser!

After a few seconds of searching for his teeth, he eventually found them! Once he put them in his mouth, he blew the whistle and people thought it was the end of the game.

Astonishingly, he blew to disallow Ebeltoft's last minute goal! The Ebeltoft players complained to him.

Erikstrup simply told them the truth. That he had wanted to end the game before they scored, but he couldn't announce because at the time he had no teeth!

Ebeltoft protested against the result to the Danish Football Association - but the country's FA stood by their referee and Norager kept their win.

A Flying Header

"Flying headers" are scored all the time in football. That is what we say when a player leaps in the air and makes contact with the football using their head.

As far as we are aware, there is only one ACTUAL flying header to have ever been scored in a game of football. And that accolade goes to an unknown seagull in Manchester, England.

At the beginning of the 1999 season, Stalybridge Celtic Colts were playing Hollingworth Juniors in a local league in the north of England.

During the game, 13-year-old striker Danny Worthington took a shot towards goal that went really high. He missed the goal by a mile - the ball went so high that it was close to hitting a cloud!

It was as the ball kept going skyward that one of the most unusual things ever seen on a football field happened.

By this point, Danny had already turned away in disgust at how rubbish his attempt on goal had been. Shoulders slumped, he was about to apologise to his teammates for the shot, when they all started running towards him. They were celebrating a goal!

Tuning back to find the ball in the back of the net, Danny put his arms in the air and joined in the celebrations too. He had no idea how the ball had ended up there, but that wasn't going to stop him from celebrating!

He turned out to be celebrating an assist.

That's right, Danny got credited with an assist and the official goal went to a random seagull that was flying over the penalty spot.

Danny's looping shot hit the seagull as the bird was swooping down. The ball bounced off the bird and into the back of the net!

Making a Dog's Dinner Out of it

You could be forgiven for thinking that birds were the only animals to score on the football pitch. However, there are countless tales of man's best friend getting on the scoresheet.

The most famous of these occasions must be the goal scored for Deportivo San Miguel de Rio Viejo during a Chilean football game in 2021.

As San Miguel lined up to take a free kick on the edge of the area, they called up their most trusted headers of the ball - most noticeably their centre backs.

What the opposition (Real Zaragoza) didn't know was that they had a secret weapon up their sleeve.

As the free kick was taken, an Alsatian cleverly beat the offside trap to head into the bottom left corner of the net - leaving Real Zaragoza's goalkeeper rooted to the spot.

A notable mention for another great pooch on a football field story must go to one of the greatest saves ever seen. One that would make even Peter Schmeichel be proud of. After all, he is the Great Dane!

The scene was Greater Glasgow, and Vale of Leven AFC and Ferguslie Star were battling it out in the AFL President's Cup match. It was a winner-takes-all affair.

Vale of Leven ended up winning the game 3-2, so you can imagine how angry Ferguslie striker Ross Hamilton was when he beat the offside trap, latched onto a long ball, and slotted past the keeper only to find his shot blocked by a dog having a good ol' sniff at the near post.

Annoyingly for Ferguslie Star, the ball rebounded off the dog and landed at the feet of one of their strikers who scored, but the referee ruled the goal out because of the dog's interference and gave the Leven goalkeeper a drop ball.

Triple Word Sore

There have been some crazy injuries in the history of football.

Like the time English international goalkeeper David Seaman got injured as he stretched for the remote controller in his bed.

Or there's the story of Danish Liverpool goalkeeper Michael Stensgaard who dislocated his shoulder as he was pulling down an ironing board. Stensgaard sadly had to retire because of this injury.

The craziest silly injury has got to go to Lionel Letiz.

In 2002 The French goalkeeper injured his back whilst playing the very physical game that is scrabble.

Yup, the very same game that great grandmothers around the world play in comfy sofas for hours on end.

As the French goalkeeper was playing the board game, a couple of tiles fell on the floor.

It was as he bent over to pick them up that he pulled some muscles in his back. He was out injured for quite some time and never really recovered to his previous best.

An honourable mention for a bizarre injury must go to Darius Vasell of England, who tried to alleviate a blister in his toe by drilling through his toenail with an electric power drill.

This was an incredibly silly thing to do, and he then had to go to hospital to get his foot fixed.

The Scorpion Kick

Football is an exciting sport, but most of the time, you roughly know what is going to happen.

Rene Higuita was a goalkeeper who didn't like it when people "roughly knew" what was going to happen during a game.

He was an entertainer trapped in a footballer's body.

He would often try and take on the opposition by himself, ball still at his feet, despite being the last person defending his goal. Something his teammates didn't like.

He wanted to entertain people so much that he also started scoring goals.
The footballing world had rarely seen a goalkeeper who would take free kicks and penalties - but Higuita made it famous. He actually scored a healthy 41 goals in his career!

With crazy hair to match his crazy personality, it was on September 6 1995, that he wrote his name into the history books. Colombia were playing England at the 'Home' of football, Wembley stadium in London. During the game, Jamie Redknapp lobbed a ball into the goalmouth - an easy catch for any goalkeeper.

"I could catch it safely..." Higuita probably thought.
Then he remembered he was an entertainer. "Nah, let's go down in history!"

Instead of catching the ball (like anyone else would), the goalkeeper decided to throw himself in front of the ball, contort himself in mid air in the shape of a scorpion, and use his 'stinger' (his two legs arching over his back) to clear the ball out of his area.

The English football commentator of the game was obviously not expecting that - "Goodness me!" he shrieked.

The next day, in every playground in every country, school children across the world were trying this move.

Never again has a keeper attempted this audacious move during a game.

The Lionesses

It is not often that a single game of football can change a whole country.

But that's exactly what happened on July 31 2022 when England beat Germany 2-1 to win the Women's European Championship.

England had gone over 50 years without any major international victories in the sport. For everyone in the country, it was 50 years too long.

When it came to football, English people were very sad.

The whole country lived with a hopeless dream that football would one day "come home".

The thing was that 'one day' didn't really seem like it was ever going to come. Until the last day of July in the summer of 2022.

The Lionesses did what no other English team had done in 56 years. They beat Germany in a final and gave England their first senior football trophy of the 21st century.

What the lionesses did for the country, and most importantly, for millions of young fans across the country was immeasurable. They united the country at a time when it was going through a bad time.

They gave everyone in the country hope, joy and pride.

At a time when a lot of people thought men's football was better than women's football, the Lionesses victory changed that forever.

Never again would women's football be seen as anything but equal to that of their male's counterpart.

A huge change to the way the country thought, and a testament to the grit, passion and determination those girls showed for their country that summer.

3
11
9

I Can't See You in Grey

On April 13 1996 Manchester United played Southampton at The Dell. At the end of the first half, United found themselves 3-0 down.

United players went into the dressing room wearing grey and came back out wearing blue and white stripes.

Their manager's idea to win the game was to change the colour of the kit that his players were wearing! He hoped that this would turn the game around and see them rescue at least a draw from the game.

The team could not recover in the second half and they were beaten by Southampton in the end.

The only thing more embarrassing than the scoreline was the excuse their manager, Alex Ferguson, made for the loss. He claimed that the players couldn't pick each other out on the pitch because of the colour of the kit - and that had been the reason why he'd ordered his troops to change kit at half time.

People laughed at the time, but apparently Ferguson had been in touch with "eye scientists" at the time.

The advice from the professionals was that grey was one of the hardest colours the human eye could see. As such Ferguson kept a second kit on standby whenever they played in grey - just in case!

On that day when United had an awful first half, Ferguson thought it was down to the kit and quickly rectified it at halftime.

The world saw it as an outrageous excuse, but, two decades later it was discovered that there was science to the madness.

Not that it mattered, United went on to lose 3-1 and were fined £10,000 by the English Football Association for changing kits at half time.

In Ferguson's defence, you could argue that they won the second half 1-0.

BECKHAM
24

Pizza-gate

Talking about Ferguson, there's a great story that originates from Old Trafford in Manchester.

The year was 2004 and Arsenal were visiting Manchester United on a run of being unbeaten for 49 games.

Arsenal players were gloating about the fact that the 50th unbeaten game would be achieved at the home of their bitter rivals. United didn't quite like that.

The game was tense and physical. Ruud Van Nistelrooy was lucky to be on the pitch after a bad challenge on Ashley Cole. He then scored a goal to add salt into Arsenal's wound.

The Gunners went on to lose their unbeaten streak and all hell broke loose after full time in the tunnel on the way back to the changing rooms.

A full fight broke out, things were surely going to get considerably out of hand when a pizza was thrown across the tunnel, landing flat on Alex Ferguson's face.

It dribbled down his cheek and onto his elegant suit. Time stood still.

Pushing people around, despite not being very nice at all, was somewhat acceptable when emotions were running high.

However, covering the most successful British manager in marinara sauce was a step too far. Ferguson retired to the changing room, and the players – feeling like they had really let down the headmaster – followed soon after.

For years after the event, the British press tried to discover who the culprit of this cowardly act had been. The investigation (creatively dubbed 'pizza-gate'), led nowhere.

It wasn't until a few years, in a radio phone interview, that Martin Keown revealed that the person who threw the pizza had been none other than Cesc Fabregas.

"I Can Give You a Hand" Literally

In 1906 in Argentina, Barracas FC lost their goalkeeper to bitter rivals Alumni FC. With an upcoming game against Estudiantes, Barracas were scrambling to find a goalkeeper.

As is often the case, one of their defenders stepped up and offered his services in between the sticks.

"I can give you a hand", Winston Coe said. "You know I can't give you two", he said jokingly. Winston Coe only had one arm.

With the game only round the corner, Barracas FC found themselves in a bit of a pickle. They had to say yes. Coe went in between the sticks for the game against Estudiantes, and both fans and players were gobsmacked by Coe's performance on the day.

The Argentinean press praised him for his confidence and shot stopping ability (apparently he saved quite a few shots that day).

Estudiantes beat Barracas 2-1 despite Coe's heroic efforts, but his performance was so good that Barracas kept him in goal for their next two games.

Unfortunately for Barracas, they went on to lose 11-0 against Reformer and 5-0 against an Alumni side that had their former goalkeeper in the team.

Imagine how he felt when he walked out onto the pitch and realised he'd been replaced with a man with one arm?!

Despite the two beatings, the Argentine press concluded that the results would have been "catastrophic" had Coe not been in goal.

With three games under his belt, Winston Coe not only taught the world a lesson in determination, he also gifted us one of the most feel-good football stories out there!

The Game of Three Halves

In the opening game of the English 1894/95 football season, referee Thomas Kirkham, was late for kick-off.

Not that it mattered. Everyone trusted a Mr. John Conqueror to take his place until the referee arrived.

It was hard not to trust him with a surname like that!

Conqueror was happy to volunteer his services, and the game between Derby County and Sunderland began.

Derby County didn't start well. They conceded 3 goals in the first 45 minutes.

Conqueror blew for half-time and handed the whistle over to Thomas Kirkham, the original referee who had arrived 45 minutes late!

It was at this point that this game would go down as one of the most incredible games in the history of the sport.

Kirkham asked the Derby team if they would not prefer to start the game from the very beginning? Losing by 3 goals, their answer was obvious.

The little boy tasked with hanging the numbers on the scoreboard had to take down the "3" under Sunderland and put up a fresh "0" under both Sunderland and Visitors.

Mr. T Kirkham started the entire 90 minutes over again!

Sunderland kept to their original game plan. So much so that by the end of the "second half", the little boy had hung up 3-0 to Sunderland once again.

The players went into the dressing room for their second half time break and came out to battle their way through a "third half".

Sunderland, fired by a sense of injustice perhaps, were ruthless. That little boy ended up hanging five more goals for Sunderland, with a 8-0 victory for the Black Cats.

8
0

Pickles The Dog And The Missing World Cup

England hosted and won the World Cup in the summer of 1966. They were also very lucky to have a trophy to lift at the end of the event.

On the 20th of March, a few weeks before the beginning of the tournament, the trophy disappeared from Westminster's Central Hall, where it had been on display to the public.

The following day, the police received a ransom note demanding £15,000 in £1 and £5 notes if they wanted the trophy back.

As the police prepared a complicated operation to get the trophy back (it included printing fake notes), an unlikely new hero emerged: Pickles the black and white collie dog.

As Pickles went for his Sunday walkies in Beulah Park, South East London on the 27th of March 1966 he stopped to sniff a package wrapped in newspaper. It was lying next to the front wheel of a parked car.

Pickles' owner, upon unwrapping it, must have been gobsmacked to discover it was the missing World Cup!

His owner received the equivalent of £100,000 in today's money as a reward for finding the trophy, but it was arguably Pickles who gained more value from the find.

Not only did Pickles get awarded the silver medal of the National Canine Defence League, but he got invited to England's celebration banquet after the team won the World Cup.

He also starred in film and television shows for the remainder of the year and won multiple "Dog of the Year" awards.

He will always be known as the dog who rescued the World Cup.

DOG
OF THE
YEAR

The Goal That Was "Like a UFO Landing"

Depending on who you ask, aliens and UFOs don't exist.

This is because they are so rare that only very few people have ever apparently seen them.

So when a manager says that a goal was "like a UFO landing," you know something extraordinary has happened!

It was September 2008 and Watford FC were playing against Reading FC.

In the 15th minute of the game at Vicarage Road, Reading fired in a corner. The play continued FIVE METRES away from the goal line, when, out of nowhere, the referee blew his whistle!

To the astonishment of everyone, the referee gave a goal to Reading. Everyone in the ground was gobsmacked (Reading players included!).

The ball had been so far away from the goalline that everyone thought the referee was joking.

When they realised he wasn't, many Watford players were very angry.

Furore ensued and the Referee red carded Aidy Boothroyd, the Watford manager, for dissent.

Watford managed to claw back the deficit to 2-1, but unfortunately a late penalty to Reading meant the match ended 2-2 (despite the ball only crossing the line 3 times).

A disgruntled Aidy Boothroyd, when questioned about the goal after the game, said: "I could not believe it. It was like a UFO had just landed."

A Very Public World Cup Poo

Gary Lineker is the English darling of football.

The ex-England-striker-turned-TV-pundit is one of the most liked presenters in England.

In fact, he is so liked that he can get away with pooing in front of 35,000 people, wiping his bottom and hands on the grass, and still going on to earn the love and admiration of his fellow countrymen and women.

It was 1990 and England were playing Ireland in a World Cup group game in Italy. Lineker had a brilliant start, scoring a goal in under ten minutes. However, unbeknownst to his fans, he was playing with an upset tummy.

In the second half he tried to control a ball that was passed in the air to him. He collapsed on the floor under a challenge from an Irish defender, and whilst sitting up on the ground, did a weird sort of 'break dance' on his bum.

He then ran to the opposition's area and wiped his hands on the grass.

This was all before continuing through to the semi finals of the World Cup, where England lost to Germany. Lineker established himself as a world class striker en route to the semi-final.

It wasn't until two decades later, that the seemingly innocuous 'break dance on his bum' that was caught by TV cameras, took on a new meaning.

Lineker confessed to the world that he couldn't control his diarrhoea that day in 1990, and he accidentally pooed himself whilst stretching for the ball.

The quick thinking attacker quickly slid on his bum to clear the mess, and did the same with his hands as he ran to receive the ensuing free kick.

It's no wonder that defenders couldn't get anywhere near him that tournament. The smell probably put them off!

The Lisbon Lions

Imagine grabbing all your neighbourhood mates for a game of football and ending up winning the biggest club competition in the world.

That's exactly what Celtic FC did in 1967.

That year Celtic won the European Cup. No biggie, right? There have been dozens of teams to have done that since.

However, what makes Celtic FC's achievement of 1967 so mind-blowingly good, is that all of their players that season were born within 30 miles of their home ground, Celtic Park.

Bobby Lennox was the person born the furthest away, and he only lived an hour away by bus!

A group of lads, all born close by, taking on and slaying European Giants, is the stuff of Hollywood films.

In the summer of 1967, the 15 Scotsmen travelled to Lisbon to line up against the mighty Inter Milan in the final of the European Cup.

The Italian giants were looking to take home yet another European Cup (having won two in the previous three finals) and took the lead in the first half.

Celtic fought back, and scored twice to beat Inter 2-1.

"There is not a prouder man on God's Earth than me at this moment", said Jock Stein, Celtic Manager on the day.

It's a pride that has continued for over 50 years Celtic Park, and one which, given the global scale of the modern game, will never be repeated again.

Villan's Villain Four Goal Fest

There are only very few things in football that are more satisfying than scoring a hat-trick. One of those things is perhaps scoring 4 goals instead of 3.

That is exactly what Chris Nicholl did for Aston Villa in 1976 when they played Leicester City at Filbert Street.

And whilst there have been many players since Nicholl who have bagged four or more goals in one game, what rocketed Nicholl into the record books is that the game he scored all four goals in ended up a 2-2 draw!

A skilled centre back, Chris Nicholl often got on the scoresheet. He is often remembered for a 25 yard screamer that he scored against Everton in the 1977 League Cup final.

However, it is the performance in the game against Leicester that will forever make him a household legend.

Twice he put the opposition in front, and twice he made amends by clawing back the deficit that he had single-handedly imposed on his team.

After the game, Nicholl asked the referee for the ball to commemorate the event. The referee politely declined as it was his only ball (how times have changed!)

Interestingly, it was not the first time a player had scored two goals and two own goals in a game.

Sam Wynne did exactly the same thing for Oldham Athletic against Manchester United back in 1923 - although that game ended up as a 3-2 Victory to Odlham!

It seems lightning can strike twice (or eight times) on a football pitch!

Football's Greatest Fairytale

A story of fantastical forces and beings, with fighters & villains, and unlikely heroes in the making. Such are the ingredients of a fairytale.

In August 2015, bookmakers across the world thought that there was more chance of finding a mythical monster in the depths of Loch Ness, than there was of Leicester City FC winning the Premier League.

Nine months later, one of those two things became a reality.

Leicester's journey started gripping the whole world around February 2016. It was at this point that the team's position in the league (they cemented the top position after beating title favourites Manchester City) could no longer be seen as a fluke.

The world was gripped - every neutral fan in the world wanted them to continue fighting against all odds, and stay top for a few more games.

The players, who had come from humble football origins, were not only competing in the toughest league in the world, they were beating the richest clubs in the world.

Week in and week out, Leicester would go on to brush aside whatever team was put in front of them, and it was clear to see that legends were being made.

Future World Cup winners like N'golo Kanté were emerging, and other talents like Riyad Mahrez were lighting up the league with their skill.

Like a soap opera that grips a nation, the feel good story continued every weekend, until May 2nd 2016, when other games in the league mathematically confirmed that Leicester City would be champions of England.

Out of the 38 fixtures that season they won 23, drew 12, and lost only three! They were the giant-killers of the decade, if not the century.

People the world over were in delirium. The most epic of underdog sagas had just been completed. To top it off, it had all been overseen by their leader Claudio Ranieri, the most charismatic old man, the kind of grandfather everyone's always wanted to have.

Zombie Footballers? The World's Longest Match

In 2019 a group of amateur football players decided to break a record for the longest football game ever played.

To do this, they played continuously in a mind-numbing and strength-sapping football match that lasted 169 hours!

That's one week and 1 hour of continuous football.

Playing football is any fan's dream, but doing anything continuously for over a week would surely test your resolve.

Tempers frayed and tears were shed in the course of the marathon, as players stumbled on for hour after hour, day after day.

But the play had to go on uninterrupted if they wanted to break the record.

The teams were aiming to beat the Guinness World record of 134 hours, but as they played, the distressing news came in that a German side had played for 168 hours.

So, they played grimly onwards for the extra day and a half.

The scoreline ended up at 988-951, and luckily for everyone involved, it was safely beyond the need for a penalty shootout!

Cancer research was the real winner at the end of the week, with the charity Kicking Off Against Cancer raising thousands of pounds through their efforts.

Blink And You'll Miss it

The quickest goal ever recorded by the English Football Association was scored by Marc Burrows.

The English striker was playing for Cowes Sports Reserves against Eastleigh when, in 2004, he took a shot immediately after kick off.

Aided by some strong winds, the shot rocketed into the back of the opposition's net an impressive 2.56 seconds after kick off.

Nawaf Al Abed of Saudi Arabia claims to have scored in 2 seconds for Al Hilal against Al Shoalah, however his time has never been officially recorded by the Guiness Book of World Records.

There is little to no video evidence of the above two goals, so an honourable mention must go to Gavin Stokes of Maryhill FC, who wins the award of 'fastest-goal-where-there-is-plenty-of-video-evidence-for'.

After the Ballon D'or, that's the most coveted award in world football.

In 2017, Maryhill FC were facing Clydebank FC in a Scottish semi-professional league.

The Clydebank goalie was still adjusting his gloves when a looping shot straight from kick off by Stokes went past his head with only 3.2 seconds on the clock.

The fastest youth goal on record was delivered in a 2012 match in Serbia, when Dorcol's Vuk Bakic teed off to score a stunner against Polet. It stopped the clock at 2.2 seconds, beating Mark Burrows' previous record score for Cowes Sports Reserves against Eastleigh by a few seconds.

Bakic's goal is also very popular on YouTube and it makes for some great viewing for everyone – apart from the opposing goalkeeper.

Most Fans in a Stadium

In 1923 Wembley Stadium hosted its first ever match: The FA Cup final between Bolton Wanderers and West Ham United.

The game drew a sell-out crowd of 126,000. However, about another 180,000 spectators made their way into the stadium.

In the end, it is estimated that there were about 300,000 human beings packed inside Wembley Stadium that late April afternoon in 1923. (300,022 if you include the players on the pitch!)

The game had to be postponed for 45 minutes as the crowd spilled onto the playing field and didn't allow play to start.

That was easily fixed by the police though, who carelessly came round on horses and crammed the pitch invaders back into the stands. Miraculously, nobody got hurt; and Bolton won their first ever FA Cup that day.

The official record for the most fans in one game, however, goes to the Maracana Stadium in Brazil. Uruguay was being hosted by Brazil for the 1950 World Cup final. Interest was at fever pitch, resulting in 199,854 people cramming into the stadium!

Twelve winners' medals had been made in advance and inscribed with the Brazilian team's names. The local press had even published a newspaper edition with the banner headline "Brazil: World Champions!!!"

Unfortunately for Brazil, Uruguay went on to win 2-1. It's safe to say that the match also holds the record for the highest numbers of sad spectators leaving a stadium.

In modern football, the largest football crowd ever recorded was in the Michigan Stadium, USA, in 2014.

The super-sized American stadium filled up with about 109,000 spectators supporting Manchester United and Real Madrid, who were competing in the International Champions Cup. A big crowd for a friendly game.

The Most Amount of Goals Ever

Fans of other sports may knock football because of its lack of goals.

If you ever have to find yourself defending the excitement of our beautiful game, then perhaps point those other sports fans to this chapter.

The biggest winning margin in a game of football was 149-0. It happened in a match played between AS Adema and SO l'Emyrne of Madagascar in 2002. The Guinness Book of Records has it down as the world's biggest ever loss, but it never really was a 'competition'.

SO l'Emyrne threw the game by deliberately scoring own goals for 90 minutes. This was in protest against a disputed refereeing decision in the previous week's game. The poor referee at that game was powerless, and had to keep on blowing for the goal and re-starting play. For a whole hour and a half.

The game was meant to be a mouth-watering showdown between two ancient rivals, so the spectators demanded their money back after the game.

The local football association banned the coach and the captain of SO l'Emyrne for the rest of the season, and both teams (unfairly for one) got a severe reprimand.

The biggest scoreline, from a match where two professional* teams were actually competing, was delivered by Arbroath FC of Scotland.

They buried the hapless Bon Accord FC under 36 goals in the 1885 Scottish Cup. Bon Accord might have been outgunned, but at least they honourably tried to play.

In the modern era, though, the biggest drubbing on record happened in the South Pacific, when American Samoa lost their World Cup qualifier to Australia by 31-0 in 2002.

It was spectacular, but hardly a footballing spectacle. Australian Archie Thompson scored a world-record 13 goals in that match.

*paid footballers didn't come until much later, but they were compensated in other ways

Bury me in my Boots - I'll Never Hang Them Up!

Many footballers love the game too much to stop playing at a reasonable age.

It is very common to see fifty-year olds routinely lumber over marshy club fields on Sunday afternoons, occasionally embarrassing younger, less skilled players with defence splitting passes.

Still, nobody can hold a candle to Ezzeldin Bahader, the world's oldest professional football player who plays for Egyptian club October 6.

On March 7 2020, Bahader became the oldest active professional football player by coming onto the pitch at the grand old age 74 years and 125 days.

He missed a penalty in a 3-2 defeat to El Ayat Sports Club, but at least entered The Guinness Book of Records.

He also dislodged a disgruntled Isaak Hayik, who at 73, had been the previous record holder.

The following year, at 75, Bahader pushed new boundaries by scoring a professional goal for October 6 playing in the derby match against El Alyat.

Despite dizziness and a wonky knee, Bahader emerged from Covid-19 lockdown to play a full 90 minutes, and this time he managed to score from the spot.

Bahader might have retired from his job as a civil engineer, but his footballing career is still going strong at the time of writing.

With six grandchildren, he is never going to be short of supporters!

Go Pops!
Proud of My Grandad!

Football's Biggest Fraudster

Ali Dia could play football - just. He was much better at telling lies.

In 1996 he started ringing football clubs lying about who was. He claimed to be George Weah, who at the time was the world's best player. When he rang the clubs, he said that he had a cousin who played football really well and was looking for a club. He was essentially trying to sell himself.

Most football clubs rightfully dismissed the call as a hoax. But the phone then rang at Southampton FC and manager Graeme Souness picked up.

A few minutes later and we imagine the conversation went something like this:
Souness: "... Lastly George, you promise he's really good?"

"George Weah": "I promise. Why would I be saying this if he wasn't?"

What followed was one of the most bizarre tales in modern football.

Grame Souness, without seeing Ali Dia ever play, and simply going off a phone conversation with someone who claimed was the best football player on the planet, signed the midfielder on a one-month long contract.

In November 1996, and despite trepidations from the Southampton squad, Souness named Dia as a substitute for their game against Leeds.

After 32 minutes, Matt Le Tissier picked up an injury. Ali Dia was thrown on as a like-for-like substitute.

It was the worst appearance by a professional in the history of the sport. Dia was disastrous.

His teammates watched on, bemused and horrified as the obviously uncoordinated Dia stumbled and miskicked and, most disastrously, left the team severely handicapped.

Leeds scored. After 82 minutes Souness had had enough, and subbed him off for a real player. The damage had been done, and Leeds ended up winners at 2-0.

A Truly Golden Goal

Tahiti is a tiny country in the middle of the Pacific Ocean.

Its national team has very few full-time footballers. Most team members work in 9am-5pm professions, and go to football practice in the evenings.

In 2012, they had a golden season. They won the Oceania Football Confederation (a regional competition) and qualified for the 2013 Confederations Cup in Brazil!

They were going to be playing against the biggest teams in the world. And the question before all the encounters was simply about how little they could lose by.

In the end, Tahiti let in 24 goals in three matches, 6 against Nigeria, 10 against Spain, and 8 against Uruguay.

The most remarkable of their feats happened in the game against Nigeria: THEY SCORED A GOAL!

A towering header by one of the Tehau brothers sent everyone watching the tournament into delirium.

Every single neutral watched through teary eyes as the Tahitan players celebrated the moment of undiluted joy - despite being comprehensively beaten.

It clearly was a goal dedicated to everyone back in their home island. The Tahitans celebrated the goal by pretending to row in a canoe - in homage to their nation's fishing heritage.

A beautiful sight to behold and probably the most cheered on goal by fans everywhere across the globe (probably even Nigerians at that point - it was that emotional).

The team returned back home as heroes, having achieved an international competition goal.

Ice Cream, You Scream, We All Scream!

Football and ice cream are two of the BEST things in the world.

Sadly, they don't often combine.

Unless, of course, you were Stockport County in the 1920s!

Back then, football wasn't played professionally. Which means that no money was paid to players or for transfers of players between clubs.

In 1927, Manchester United liked the look of a certain player called Hugh McLenahan - he was playing for Stockport County.

United really wanted Stockport County to give them McLenahan. But as money wasn't allowed to be traded, they needed to come up with a different idea, an offer they couldn't refuse.

So United's assistant manager Luis Rocca, whose family business was in the ice cream industry, donated two freezers full of ice cream to Stockport County's fund-raising bazaar in exchange for McLenahan's services.

TWO FULL FREEZERS OF ICE CREAM!

No sane person in the world would refuse that offer! Stockport obviously accepted the offer, and off he went to play for United.

ICE-CREAM
ICE-CREAM

The Greatest Cup Run in The World

The story of Calais Racing Union FC is the Cinderella equivalent of amateur football fairy tales.

Some of the best feel-good stories in football are when part-time football players beat professional football players. But if there's one way to make a feel-good story feel even better, it's when the footballers who defeat the pros aren't part-timers, but complete amateurs.

That's exactly what happened in the 1999/2000 Coupe de France when Calais Racing Union had the best cup run any amateur side has ever seen. Their amazing run saw them beat Bordeaux in the semi-final and reach the final.

It was so exciting that even their manager had a minor heart attack and had to be briefly hospitalised! The president of France, Jacques Chirac, rang him up in hospital that evening to make sure he was OK.

The amateurs went onto the final at Stade De France, which had only recently been the venue for another final - the World Cup final!

Only Nantes stood between Calais and arguably the single greatest football story ever. Calais took the lead in the 34th minute of the game. We were about to see the unthinkable...

Unfortunately that's where the fairy tale stopped. Nantes went on to score two goals and win the game.

At the trophy presentation, the Nantes captain invited the Calais captain to accompany him. They lifted the trophy together in one of the most beautiful scenes competitive football had ever seen.

Calais had gained the hearts of the French nation - they were well and truly the people's champions.

Would you like Book 02 for free?

Reviews are critical to my career as an author! They serve as the foundation to my success.

I'm so committed to this belief that I'd like to offer you **a free copy** of the second book in the series, 'The Most Amazing Soccer Stories Of All Time - For Kids.'

Simply email me at mikelangdon1@gmail.com with the Subject line: FREE MASS02.

I'll personally respond to your email to arrange the best shipping address for your book.

Take a sneak peek at the book in the following pages!

Did you enjoy these stories?

Your journey doesn't end here!

Click on the QR code below to grab Book 2 of 'The Most Amazing Soccer Stories Of All Time!'

Your next soccer adventure awaits!

SCAN ME

There's a sneak peek of Book 2 waiting for you on the following pages!

The crowning of The GOAT

Once upon a time, in the land of Qatar, the stage was set for the crowning of the soccer king - The Greatest Of All Time.

Lionel Messi was undoubtedly the best soccer player in the world, but to truly earn the title of The GOAT, he needed to win one specific trophy: The FIFA World Cup.

As his soccer superpowers were starting to wane, the 2022 World Cup was his final chance to win the prestigious event that only comes around once every four years. The weight of 45 million Argentineans rested squarely on his shoulders, and the pressure to perform well was immense.

Despite losing his first match, Messi's talent and perseverance shone through as he went on to score a goal at every stage of the World Cup. He single-handedly carried his team all the way to the final.

The final was the greatest the world had ever seen. The game ended in a 3-3 draw with France, and Messi scored two of the six goals. As the game ended in a draw, it had to be decided on penalties.

Lionel Messi's 20 years of tricks, goals, and mesmerizing dribbles were about to be recognized as the best ever, but only if the last penalty kick went in. His teammate Gonzalo Montiel stood on the penalty spot, and it all came down to that one kick of a soccer ball.

Montiel scored, and Messi, who was in the center circle, collapsed on his knees crying tears of joy. He had finally been crowned as the King of the Soccer World - the undoubted Greatest Of All Time.

10
10

More sendings off than players on the field!

The scenes that followed Argentina's World Cup triumph after Lionel Messi's performance in 2022, showed us that the South American country is full of very passionate soccer people.

Sometimes this passion can be shown in moments of happiness or in moments of frustration.

Unfortunately for the teams of Claypole and Victoriano Arenas, their players were very passionately frustrated after a game in 2011.

After the game against Claypole, Victoriano Arenas players were not happy when the full time whistle was blown, and the mother of all fights broke out in the center circle. And it wasn't just the 22 players on the pitch getting involved.

Not wanting to be left out, along came the substitutes and the coaching staff of both teams to show their frustration.

Legend has it that even the bus drivers of the opposing teams got involved in the action!

In the aftermath of the storm, referee Damian Rubino walked into the dressing room of both teams to individually send off every single member of staff in each team.

That amounted to 36 red cards in total, and a Guinness Book of World Records award for the most sendings off in a single game of soccer!

The Hand of God

In 1986 England and Argentina met in the World Cup. Tensions were still running high from a war they had fought 4 years earlier.

The game was a knock-out quarter final game and two of the most remarkable things in World Cup history happened over the course of the following 90 minutes.

In the first half, a young Diego Maradona waltzed around the English back line before trying to play a one-two with his team mate. Maradona was so good that he got the English defender to play the one two for him - the defender accidentally looping the ball into the 6 yard box.

English goalkeeper Peter Shilton was just about to punch the ball away, when the little Argentinian magician jumped up and used his hand to nudge the ball into the back of the net.

An illegal move that was so audacious in nature that everyone in the ground was wondering why he was crazy enough to celebrate it like he was.

The problem was that the referee didn't spot the infringement and allowed the goal to stand.

Maradona didn't wait too long to admit his guilt. After the match he said it wasn't his hand that scored the goal, but rather "the hand of God".

To make matters worse for the English, four minutes later Maradona danced his way around half a dozen English players before slotting the ball past the English goalkeeper.

It was one of the most beautiful sights global soccer has ever seen. True poetry in motion. It became known as "The Goal of the Century".

It was something for the Argentineans to celebrate after a decade of disagreements with the English.

By The Same Author

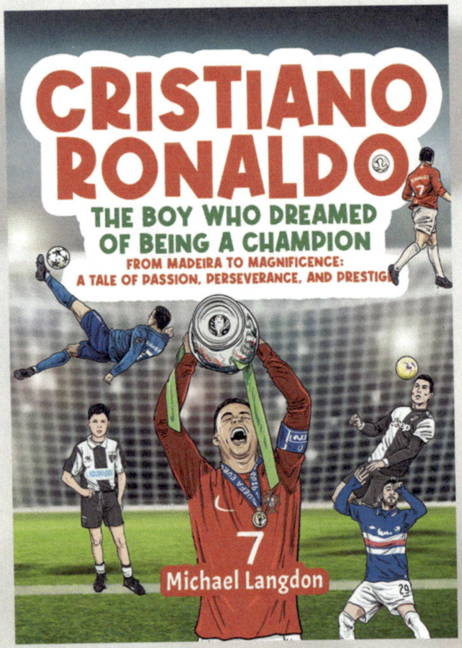

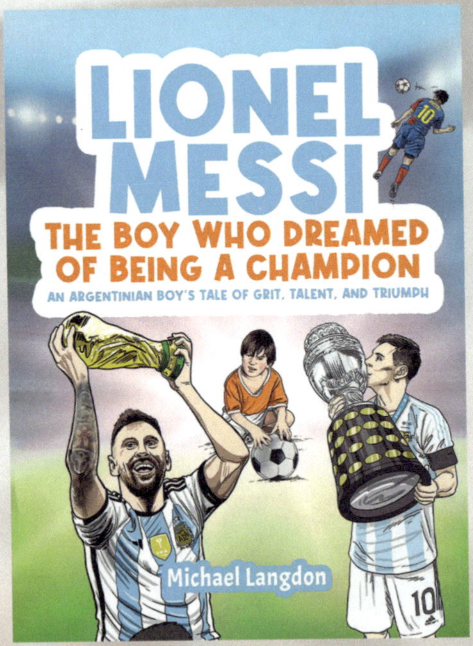

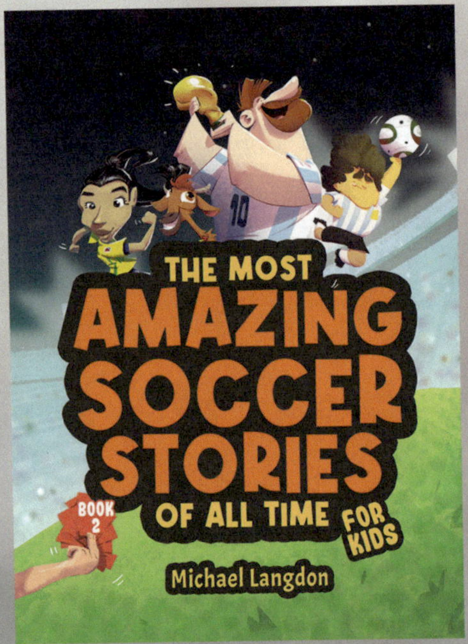

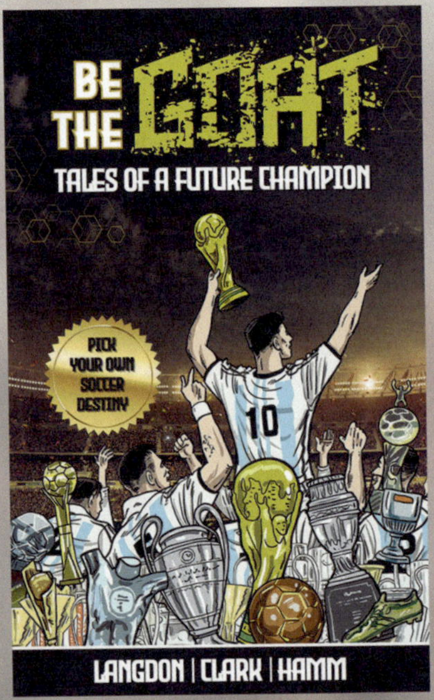

THE MOST
AMAZING
SOCCER
STORIES
OF ALL TIME
FOR KIDS!
MICHAEL LANGDON
SCAN ME

Made in the USA
Columbia, SC
05 February 2025

53409953R00043